SANT GIANI KARTAR SINGH BHINDRANWALE

ISHWAR SINGH

Copyright © Ishwar Singh
All Rights Reserved.

This book has been published with all efforts taken to make the material error-free after the consent of the author. However, the author and the publisher do not assume and hereby disclaim any liability to any party for any loss, damage, or disruption caused by errors or omissions, whether such errors or omissions result from negligence, accident, or any other cause.

While every effort has been made to avoid any mistake or omission, this publication is being sold on the condition and understanding that neither the author nor the publishers or printers would be liable in any manner to any person by reason of any mistake or omission in this publication or for any action taken or omitted to be taken or advice rendered or accepted on the basis of this work. For any defect in printing or binding the publishers will be liable only to replace the defective copy by another copy of this work then available.

I am dedicating this book to the life of Giani Kartar Singh Ji
Bhindranwale.

Contents

Foreword

Ishwar Singh have more than ten years of experience in writing story books, sakhis of devotional saints and in research activities. He is a tremendous writer. He is doing excellent job by writing about the brief history of Sant Giani Kartar Singh Bhindranwale. He had shown very keen interest in the field of religious resources and other cultural issues.

He is also a very excellent teacher and also having deep knowledge about the social science issues. I have always seen him working very hard for his various books. He just want to express about the Indian culture to our new generations in a simple and brief manner. I wish him all the very best for his new book.

Birinder Pal Kaur

Preface

This book is about the brief history of Sant Giani Kartar Singh Bhindranwale. The task behind to publish such content is to spread knowledge about the unsung heroes of the Sikh history among the new generation. In the schools, which are being organised by Sikh trusts, the students are just getting very limited knowledge about the Sikh warriors. Baba Banda Singh Bahadur, Baba Deep Singh etc. are the common names on the tongues of the students but they don't know about the others. This is just an effort to spread this brief information among new generations. I hope that you will like this book.

Acknowledgements

Writing a book is harder than I thought and more rewarding than I could have ever imagined. None of this would have been possible without my best friend, my teacher, my best motivator, my beloved mother Amarjit Kaur. She was the first who inspired me for my goals and taught me various subjects and created my interest specially in Social Sciences. She stood by me during every struggle and all my successes. Whatever I had achieved in my life it is due to my mother.

I'm eternally grateful to my father Pal Singh, who took in an extra mouth to feed when he didn't have to. He taught me discipline, tough love, manners, respect, and so much more that has helped me succeed in life. I truly have no idea where I'd be if he hadn't given me a roof over my head whom I desperately needed at that age.

To my father-in-law Narinder Singh for their moral support during the up and downs in my life. He taught me how to live positive even in the worst situations by sharing his personal experiances. He is the man who suggest me to write a book in your life because it will be your book by which you will be remembered in future.

To Dr. Davinder Singh, who never saw my age, my race, or my lack of formal education. He just saw a kid hungry to learn, hungry to grow, and hungry to succeed in teaching. He never stopped me; he only encouraged me.

Prologue

India is a country of huge cultural diversities. This diversity has its roots in the ancient and medieval period of the history. In present day life, every one is playing his role according to the role assingned by the nature. I have very much interest to explore various great warriors or personalities and cultural aspects of our Indian Society. So an idea came in my mind to explore the brief history of Sant Giani Kartar Singh Bhindranwale. In this book, I have focused on the various achievements of Sant Giani Kartar Singh Bhindranwale. I am writing this book for our younger generations so that when they will read this book, they must understand the sacrifices and struggles of our forefathers.

CHAPTER ONE

Sant Giani Kartar Singh Bhindranwale

Sant Kartar Singh Jee Khalsa was born in the village of Purane Poore, Tehsil Kasoor, District Lahore in 1932 AD to Mata Labh Kaur and Jathedar Chanda Singh Ji. The location is now in the district of Amritsar. Sant Kartar Singh Ji first received his education at the Government Middle School in Khemharan. He then attended the National High School in Bhikhivind for his ninth and tenth grades before continuing his education at Khalsa College in Amritsar.

Sant Kartar Singh Ji received Gurmat instruction from Baba Baga Singh Ji, who lived in their hamlet, in addition to a general education. By Guru Ji's help, he swiftly memorised his five morning prayers, Reharas Kirtan Sohela. When they got Amrit from Sant Gurbachan Singh Ji's Jatha in Bhindran in 1948 AD, they were still enrolled in school. They developed a deep relationship with Sant Gurbachan Singh Ji after consuming Amrit.

They used to spend all of their time studying at Khalsa College engaged in Simran and devotion. In addition to the mandatory Nitnem for Sikhs, they used to recite a lot of Gurbani. At the age of 18, he performed his Anand Karaj in 1950. Shaheed Bhai Amrik Singh Jee and Bhai ManJeet

Singh Jee, two sons, were born. Sant Kartar Singh Jee initially worked as a Patwari (a village revenue official who keeps track of land holdings, conducts crop surveys, and calculates land revenue) with Khalsa Jee's approval and to fulfil his father's wish. However, in 1957 AD, he quit his position and moved permanently into the Jatha. For a while, they performed the service of serving as Khalsa Jee's Garveye (a role akin to personal assistant). Daily, they would chant the five Jaitsri Di Var Satte Balvade di Vaar 25 Ang prayers from the Sri Guru Granth Sahib Jee, and in the presence of Khalsa Jee, they would recite the Panj Granthi (It is a Pothi having Shabads from different texts of Sikhism along with Gurbani), including the Barah Maha and numerous Japjee Sahibs. They were devoted to their seva and were eager to perform any seva.

He used to spend his days immersed in Simran and Gursikhi Parchar, constantly thinking about the Sikh people (Chardhi Kala of the Sikh Nation). They would constantly question why Sikhs were departing from Sikhi, wondering whether they had forgotten the steps taken by the Guru for our welfare. He would talk about the best course of action to follow to ensure that the Sikhi message may reach every household with knowledgeable Gursikhs. Their regular schedule consisted of working until 12 or 1 AM and then waking up at 4 AM. He once said, "God has provided us with magnificent bodies, he gives us delicious food, and most importantly, he has blessed us with birth into a Sikh household. If we are tired or lethargic, we do not have the right to live—as we should be dedicating every breath to Sikhi Parchar."

When more Katha was done during the day while touring and performing Parchar, they used to feel ecstatic and energised. He used to express what a wonderful sight it would be if we could see Singhs in all directions because they had such a deep love for Sikhi that they wanted everyone to take Amrit and become Sikhs. Bookings for Sant Kartar Singh Jee were extremely difficult to come by because of the high demand. Sant Jee never turned anyone away at Gurdwara Nabha Sahib they became very ill and the Singhs had to help them up the stairs after that sangat from Chandigarh came at 10PM and said that there is a Diwan taking place and the whole sangat is waiting for your presence - even if you attend and speak for only 10 minutes. The Singhs sought to persuade Sant Jee not to go due to poor health but they still went to Chandigarh.

He once asserted that a Parcharak's lifestyle must be outstanding and disciplined for Sikhi to develop. In light of this, they emphasised that Amritdhari status was required for anyone speaking in public at the Gurdwara from the platform. He gave this advice to the Sri Patna Sahib committee, who thereafter issued an edict/Hukamnama declaring it, making 36 Dhadi Jathas and several Parcharaks Amritdahri. Sant Kartar Singh Jee delightedly offered these Parcharaks saropas at Bir Baba Budha Sahib Jee on October 7, 1976. Out of 250000 people gathered, 5000 men rose to their toes when Sant Jee told the story of Sri Guru Tegh Bahadar Jee and other Shaheeds and pledged never to drink alcohol or cut their hair ever again. When someone used to request their presence at their home and they were Patit (behaving improperly according to the Sikh Code of Conduct), cut their hair, drank alcohol, or used intoxicants, they would refuse to go there or consume anything from them until the home owners made a commitment to stop doing those things. They led many people to Sikhi in this way.

In order to commemorate Sri Guru Tegh Bahadurs Jee's 300th Shaheedhi Day, Sant Jee invited organisations and Jathebandhis Colleges to join in Sikhi preaching. Regarding this, 37 significant parades were held in various areas throughout the government's period of emergency, the accomplishments of which defy description. The whole Sikh world was awakened by these big occurrences. Sant Jee will perform Parchar while standing for a continuous 15 hours. In a 100 km long march, Sant Jee would perform parchar for ten to fifteen minutes at each village as it passed through 60 to 70 villages. The following slogan was required to be sung by the Sangat in each village:

May my head be cut off, but not at the expense of my Sikhi. Sant Jee responded that the two ministers should be made aware that the parade is being held in remembrance of and in honour of Hind dee Chadar, the Hindu people's defender. The ministers should take off their shoes, fold their hands, and stand with their hands together to make room for the congregation to pass. When Sant Jee came in Ludhiana, about 15 to 20 men stood up in the diwan to welcome him. Sant Jee had been called to lay the cornerstone of the Sri Guru Tegh Bahadur charitable hospital. Sant Jee got up and walked away. Sant Jee was questioned why he was leaving, to which he responded, "In the presence of Sri Guru Granth Sahib Jee, no-one should stand to welcome or respect another as this diminishes the dignity of the Guru." Sant Jee sent the organisers back into the diwan after they had all begged for mercy and entered by himself after them. No matter how well-known a leader or accomplished a Gursikh is, according to Sant Jee, nobody is better than the Sri Guru Granth Sahib Jee.

On December 7, 1975, in Delhi, to honour the 300th anniversary of Sri Guru Tegh Bahadur Jee's Shaheedi in the Ram Lila Ground, a procession of 2.2 million people gathered. P.M. Indira Gandhi then stepped onto the stage, and in the presence of Sri Guru Granth Sahib Jee, all those on the stage stood to welcome and honour her. However, Sant Kartar Singh Jee was the only person who remained seated. Sant Jee protested vehemently over this anti-Sikh deed on stage. Many of the speakers on stage praised P.M. Indira Gandhi for her strong relations with Punjab, which she cemented by addressing Sri Guru Tegh Bahadur Jee on behalf of the Delhi government (here the Delhi government means the central government and Delhi legislative assembly does not exists in 1975). Sri Guru Tegh Bahadur Jee is revered and respected by the same Delhi government that received information about the Sikhs.

After Prime Minister Indira Gandhi, it was Sant Jee's turn to speak, and he started out by making some insightful observations.

"In the beginning, Rajput Kings would gift their girls as prizes. If they do the same today, Sikhs will bring shame upon themselves. It is prohibited for Sikhs to marry their daughters to Monas or Patits for this reason.

They clarified a second issue, saying, "We want to know how Indira Gandhi came to rule the Delhi government. You haven't done anything particularly heroic by coming here to pay homage to Sri Guru Tegh Bahadur. If Guru Jee hadn't suffered martyrdom, a Muslim would have sat on this throne, and everyone would have been greeted with Salema Lekham. You would have been covered by a Burka.

In light of the P.M.'s body hair count, even if she were to repeatedly chop off her head and prostrate herself at Guru Jee's feet, she would not be able to pay off her obligation to Sri Guru Tegh Bahaur Jee.

No one is more powerful than our Guru, regardless of how strong the P.M. may be. She ought to make a prostration before our beloved Sri Guru Granth Sahib Jee, the light of the Ten Gurus, rather than expecting us to stand up and show her respect. Immediately after, Jakaras could be heard across the entire arena.

Sant Kartar Singh Jee's candour caused problems to be brought up by P.M. Indira Gandhi with the Damdami Taksal. No matter who they were, Sant Jee never accepted anyone disrespecting Sri Guru Granth Sahib Jee. As a result, they campaigned against the Nakali Nirankaris' assault on Sikhi and spoke out against them.

Sant Ji was in the Malseea Village. Sant Ji received a benti from a Singh requesting their trip to Shimla. Sant Ji claimed that Sant Giani Gurbachan Singh Ji Khalsa had not given them permission to travel to Shimla, but the Singh kept making benti gestures to Sant Ji. Eventually, Sant Ji informed the Singh that they would be travelling to Shimla. Sant Giani Gurbachan Singh Ji Khalsa Bhindranwale once remarked to Sant Giani Kartar Singh Ji Khalsa Bhindranwale that although life is short, there will be a lot of work to be done at that time.

Bhai Gurmukh Singh Ji Garvai was sitting in the car next to Sant Ji. During the trip, Sant Ji convinced the driver to halt the vehicle, at which point he switched seats with Bhai Gurmukh Singh Ji Garvai. Sant Ji was seriously hurt in a car accident on the way to Ludhiana, but Bhai Gurmukh Singh Ji Garvai was unharmed. The car ran off the pavement. After being brought to the C.M.C. hospital in Ludhiana, Sant Ji requested that some Singhs go get Sant Giani Jarnail Singh Ji Khalsa. The Gurbani was recited for Sant Giani Kartar Singh Ji Khalsa in the hospital by Sant Giani Jarnail Singh Ji Khalsa.

Sant Ji's family informed the medical personnel that they would pay whatever it took to ensure Sant Ji's recovery when all the Akali leaders visited him there. However, the physicians advised that they would need to do surgery and remove some of Sant Ji's hair. The physicians can remove their skull, but they cannot remove any of their hair, Sant Ji stated while stroking their palm over their chest. Sant Ji forbade anyone from shaving their body hair, not even to heal their wounds. On August 16, 1977, Sant Giani Kartar Singh Ji Khalsa Bhindranwale passed away.

During his eight years as the Jathedar of Damdami Taksal, Sant Kartar Singh Jee performed a great deal of Gurmat Parchar. They were cremated at the Gurdwara Gurdarshan Parkash in Mehta, which they had erected in honour of Sant Gurbachan Singh Jee Khalsa, on August 21, 1977.